SO LONG
DESIRED

JAMES FALCONER KIRKUP. Ever since a boy terrified of the British, has lived abroad most of his life in most of the countries of Europe, in North Africa, the USA and the Far East, where he has been living off and on since 1959. At present Professor of Comparative Literature at Kyoto University of Foreign Studies. Poet, translator, dramatist, librettist and novelist (*The Love of Others*). Latest works are *Ecce Homo: My Pasolini*; *No More Hiroshimas*; *The Guitar Player of Zuiganji* (Kyoto Editions) and *The Sense of the Visit* (Sceptre Press). His *kabuki* opera, *An Actor's Revenge*, written with Japanese composer Minoru Miki, was performed at the Old Vic in 1979, and has since been translated into Japanese for presentation in Tokyo (1984) after successful performances in the US. Kirkup's books are all being translated into Japanese, the most recent being his 'autobiography of infancy' *The Only Child* (Takumi Shoten, Tokyo) with many of the family photographs first revealed in his collection of autobiographical poems, *To The Ancestral North* (Asahi Press, Tokyo).

JOHN McRAE was born in Perth, Scotland. Studied in Glasgow and Nottingham. Has lived with his partner Jeremy Hunter in Pozzuoli, on the Bay of Naples, since 1974. He works in the new University of Basilicata, and travels constantly lecturing, reciting and acting all over Europe and the US. He has written or edited some twenty books, mostly on English literature and drama, including the definitive English edition of *Teleny*, by Oscar Wilde and others (GMP, 1986). *As It Happened* is his first collection of poetry.

GAY VERSE

SO LONG DESIRED

poems by
James Kirkup
and
John McRae

Gay Verse from GMP, the Gay Men's Press
Series editor: Martin Humphries

This collection, world copyright © 1986 GMP Publishers Ltd
Fellow Feelings, world copyright © 1986 James Kirkup
As It Happened, world copyright © 1986 John McRae
This edition first published in November 1986 by
GMP Publishers Ltd, PO Box 247, London N15 6RW, England
GMP books are distributed in the United States of America by
Subterranean Company, PO Box 10233, Eugene, Oregon 97440.

British Library Cataloguing in Publication Data

Kirkup, James
 So long desired: poems.
 1. English poetry—20th century
 I. Title II. McRae, John III. Humphries,
 Martin
 821'.912'08   PR1224
 ISBN 0-85449-038-8

Photosetting by Wilmaset, Birkenhead, Wirral
Printed and bound by the Guernsey Press Company Ltd

James Kirkup

Fellow Feelings

to the memory of Alan Turing

•

Prologue: My Gay Carnivals
Sketches for an Autobiography
Because it was He, Because it was Me
Romantic Friendships
Indian Love Lyric
To a Passer-by
God in Guatemala
Elegy for Pier Paolo Pasolini
Ecce Homo
Divina Commedia
Pasolini Agonistes
On Pasolini's *'Teorema'*
City of AIDS
Homo in Omnibus
Come Together!
Ode to Male Masturbation
Hymn to the Foreskin
Camping Out
Japanese Homomovies
Narkissos
Epilogue: All I Know Is

Introduction

'Fellow Feelings' consists of 21 poems covering many of the concerns evident in James Kirkup's work. The five poems on Pasolini come from 'Ecce Homo – My Pasolini', a book of poems and translations brought out by Kyoto Editions on the 60th anniversary of Pasolini's birth. As do 'My Gay Carnivals, 'All I Know Is', 'To a Passer-By' and 'God in Guatemala'. The remainder of the poems come from a larger and, as yet, unpublished collection entitled 'My Blue Period'.

Two connected themes of love/sex and the 'personal is political' run through the poems. At times the themes are woven together as in 'Beloved Enemy', 'Elegy for Pier Paolo Pasolini' or 'City of AIDS'. Whilst poems such as 'Romantic Friendships', 'Homo in Omnibus' or 'Camping Out' bring out one theme more strongly than another.

The explicitly sexual poems such as 'Ode to Male Masturbation' or 'Hymn to the Foreskin' are a joyous celebration of the pleasures of sex. Such expression has often been frowned upon and James Kirkup is seen as a controversial writer because his work has come into conflict with the forces of repression. In his poetry he expresses truths and realisms about the world as he sees it. Like many another before him he has been rejected for doing this and in turn he has rejected 'Thingland' as he calls this country. Like others who present us with truths we have no desire to hear he has found greater success abroad than in his native land. Perhaps 'Fellow Feelings' will, in part, redress the balance.

His poems have much to say, much to offer and much to give. They are written from the heart to be received by the heart as well as the head. Strong, shocking, simple, salutary and shameless they sing of many things. But above all they sing of life and of how 'love is the only way/to defeat the merchants of death'.

Martin Humphries
1986

My Gay Carnivals

In sunny Venice, masked,
we danced all day and night.

Now snow quilts the Sound.
The Little Mermaid
wears a white modesty-vest,
her hands frozen fish fingers,
her tail in the deepfreeze of Lent.

All alone, and lost, an only child
orphaned at the age of fifty-six,
I press my masked face against
the locked gates of Tivoli –
and the dancers are all fled.

After my gay carnivals,
bloody Easter.

Copenhagen, March 22, 1979

Sketches for an Autobiography

Giving a Reading: A Memory of the 'Fifties

I had been invited by the Oxford Poetry Society,
the usual bunch of young literary thugs
agitated by ravening ambitions,
to 'give a reading'.

In my innocent youth, and needing the money,
I asked for nothing better.
They paid for a night at the Mitre.
And there was also a free dinner.

So I went, in a fluster of trepidation and horror,
to confront unkindness, the University nitwits
lapped in the satisfactions of British complacency.
– Being born a Geordie didn't help.
We are the untouchables of Britain
in the dreary ghetto of Tyneside.

I tried to disguise the torment of that dinner
with both silence and inconsequential chatter.
After the first course, I heard a cool young voice
of a rising undergrad literary 'star'
sitting almost opposite me,
announcing to the table at large that
'he's as queer as a coot, and
doesn't care who knows it.'

The intent was humorous,
but also to humiliate their guest.
I should have risen without a word
and left them to their food and drink
and taken the first train back to London.

But in those days I was hardly aware
of being different from others.
I was bisexual as the next man; and so
I might have cared, being classed as
something else, in one ignorant generalization.

So, as in my childhood, I took no notice,
and went on chatting, trying to eat.
After the coffee,
I was allowed a few moments to myself.
I should have just left.
The insult from that silly pig
had set the tone for the evening,
and I could sense unpleasantness coming.

But to run away would have been
to make myself as despicable as they.
So, for an hour or so,
in a state of complete oblivion,
I 'gave a reading.'

Yes, I read my poems,
and they were my only friends.

Beloved Enemy

Towards the end of the war,
I, a dissidecadent, a pacifist among
a nation of heroes, was set to work
in fields and forests
with other prisoners of war –
blond, gloomy German boys and
lyrical, happy-go-lucky Italians.

Totally incompetent with axe and hoe,
and bored silly by rural life,
I had been bandied from pillar to post,
from one labour camp to another
by the War Agricultural Executive Committee
or by the Forestry Commission;
nobody wanted such an awful muff.

I had the ability, however,
to detach myself from compost heaps,
drains, potato clamps and pig-sties –
from anything that might be considered
part of the 'war effort', and,
in my own dreamy but effective way,
cultivated my own peculiar gardens.
Without knowing it, I was subversive.

Those enemies, prisoners of the British,
were my only friends.
I could speak their languages
in more senses than one.
I became one of them, and they protected me
against our war-maddened Fascist foremen
like Jock the Scot, and all the fat-arsed men
from the offices of the Forestry Commission
who would stand over me, gloating, commanding me
'to get stuck into it' as I dithered with spade or axe.

Those foreigners – I was no more foreign than they –
were my only friends, and sometimes lovers.
In a life without women,
some of them turned to one another,
and some of them to me.
We would keep a lookout for the overseer
while couples made love among the stacks
of pit-props, or behind a haystack –
Germans with Germans, Italians with Italians,
and both with me, the British blond.
They told me I reminded them
of the 'little princesses', Margaret, Elizabeth.

All good things come to an end.
The war in Europe was over,
and I could walk openly with my enemies
down Oxford's 'Gummistrasse'.

Then they went back home,
to wives, girl-friends, families,
and some to boyhood passions.
And I was left alone, more than ever
a foreigner in my own country.

It was then I decided to leave my native land
for ever, as soon as I got the chance.
My former lovers still kept writing to me –
Bimbo, Katze, Manfred, Felix, and that
'holy terror', Boni Bevilacqua
(known as 'distillata') who escaped twice, and was
   caught twice. During interrogation,
he did not betray my name, for I had helped him.

As years went by, I found them all again
at the movies, in the films and books
of Pier Paolo Pasolini, his ragazzi di vita –
Marcello, Agnolo, Rocco, Aldo, Tommasino –
and my Germans, later, in the works
of Fassbinder. In any other war,
I would do the same: love is the only way
to defeat the merchants of death.

Because it was He: Because it was Me

Love Song

Out of all the millions who pass us by
without a word, without a look,
why was it he alone who came to me,
turning a blank page in the book
of loneliness that is a human heart?
Why was it he? How did it start?
Why was it you? How did it start?

Something about us seems to give the clue
to strangers, prompts repulsion, love, hate –
but nearly always cold indifference.
What was the common sign that sealed our fate?
So many pass us by – as we, too,
pass by. What was it guided me, and you?
What was it guided me, and you?

Why did you look at me, and pause,
then smile, and speak, and take my hand?
Why did I feel my soul, and yours,
long lost, unite? How did we grow to understand
our strange encounter had to be?
– Because it was he? Because it was me?
Yes. Because it was me. Because it was he.

(Duet for either two male voices, or for
one male and one female voice.)

Romantic Friendships

Love between men in its most candid form –
a devotion, a passionate attachment
to a single man, and lasting all one's life.
A steady adoration, a constant joy
in the other's presence, in his words, his laughter,
in his weaknesses as in his strengths, his loyal heart
as much as in the warmth of purest intimacy –
spiritual and unoppressive, tender yet not clinging.

A genius, a rascal, a saint, an ordinary man –
he can be any one of these, and many more.
Age does not matter: youth in love with youth,
old with old, the aged with the young,
the teenager with the boy next door, the teammate,
classmate, the couple in their middle years,
the postman and the parson, the policeman and the
  poet –
all may know and reverence the true romance

of friendship, mutual respect, the constancy of shared
experience, and every day discover, hand in hand,
their personal uniqueness, the lost security of love,
of thoughtfulness, of correct concern and care
one for the other – that sense of being together
they cannot find with any other man. All this
  perfection
without that comical 'exchange of body fluids'
the AIDS advisors so solemnly have warned us of.

Love between men in its most candid form –
what need for the impermanent exchanges of casual
  sex
when with an embrace, a smile, a kiss in play
we can be passionately chaste, and chastely gay?

Indian Love Lyric

Male hands I loved beside the Shalimar,
where are you now? Who lies beneath your spell?
Though now grown somewhat old and fat,
or wrinkled and arthritic,
still in my heart your touch will ever dwell.

When, as we strolled along the palmy shore,
those eloquent long fingers just brushed mine,
and then entwined with them, a spark
of unknown passion seemed to leap between . . .
Brown hand in white, pale arm on amber hip,

rose-mooned fingertips upon my throbbing breast,
speechless we wandered through the scented dark
of gardens: and there, beneath a flowering of stars,
your hands caressed my hair, received my kiss,
and sought my secret love with tender violence.

You offered up your own rich mysteries
to my ecstatic lips, to my adoring gaze,
to realize a love begotten by despair
upon impossibility, a conjunction consummated
despite the opposition of the stars.

– Each year since then, I go to seek for you
along the Goan beaches, by the Ganges' side,
or on the houseboats of Kashmir, my passage to
another India, not Forster's, Ackerley's, Tagore's:
rather the mysterious realism of Jhabvala.

And still I find you there, male hands I love,
still young, and fresh, and kind, and fragrant –
but not those first devoted fingers nor the grace
that were revealed to me so many years ago
in batteries of alluring sense.

– Male hands I loved beside the Shalimar,
where are you now? Who lies beneath your spell?
Into what boughs, casting the body's vest aside,
do you and he now glide, beneath whose other spell?
Or in what other, darker garden do you lie?

To a Passer-by

(after Baudelaire)

. . . O toi que j'eusse aimé, ô toi qui le savais!

All around him roared the crowded street. But he
strode unconcerned, as in a shell of silence –
pale, sombre, all in rags, an outcast,
his thin hand sweeping his dusty hair.

Loose-limbed, slim-flanked, a statue in motion.
– I drank him in, from head to foot,
and back to head again – those smouldering eyes
that barely smiled, a murderous recognition.

Then gone – engulfed in the indifferent crowd
that could not see the wonder I had glimpsed
and never hope to see again, unless in hell –

who knows – perhaps in paradise – but always
somewhere far removed from here, this empty
   street . . .
– O, you, whom I might have loved! – You who
   desired me!

God in Guatemala

I was looking down from the terrace of the Grand
 Hotel
at the mountain torrent blundering below
through boulders big as legendary beasts,
and I saw the native labourer working on the new
stone bridge, as I had seen him every day –
naked to the waist, slim-flanked, the chest deep,
broad shoulders brown, the biceps beautiful with
 velvet dust,
a noble head with proud Aztec nose, the eyes I love in
 pits of dark,
the blue-black hair bound round the temples, pale with
 stone powder –
one I had always admired for his idle elegance
and lonely sadness, singing to himself,
working, like a poet, all alone, in poverty,
a craftsman in his leisure and his slow perfection –
and impossibly longed-for in the pure male
 unawareness of his grace.

> How lovely all those loves, so long desired
> but resisted, unfulfilled by sweet self-abnegation
> for the sake of pure delight,
> of memory untainted by regret or disillusion!
> I treasure all such loves of mine.

Like this one. Every morning he was there, at dawn,
washing his face in the candid mountain stream,
rinsing his godlike nakedness in one deep, secret
 mountain pool
that I alone shared with him.

And every morning he offered me the darkness of his smile
lit with the sunshine of teeth like a mouthful of rice,
the black eyes fizzing with fun in their long black lashes.
Every morning he gave me the smile of purest friendship
as I walked to the wakening village, the forest
or the ancient church, in ruins, like an abandoned cairn.

And all we ever said at first was silences;
then just 'Buenas' or 'Hola' – the simplest words of love.
– But suddenly, this morning, as I looked down upon him from
the air-conditioned cloud of my luxury tourist suite, I wept
for the bitter pang of true and unrequited love, for him
who was oblivious of my gaze, my name, my whole existence.

And I wondered, against my will –
can God, unknown and inexistent, gaze
on me, the unbeliever, with love and understanding and concern
as I gaze now upon my brother – can He
safer bitter pain like this at my
indifference and ignorance?
And can that unknown labourer and I, despite ourselves,
be sheltered by a common grace?

– I pray so, for both our sakes.

Volcano Fuego

Elegy for Pier Paolo Pasolini

(murdered, Rome, November 2nd, 1975)

So Momma Roma got you in the end –
the bitch goddess and her instrument,
a bit of teenage rough trade, one of those
subproletarian ragazzi di vita you immortalized
in poetry and film – one of your own sorry passions.

Sex for you, as for so many of us,
was pure pleasure, uncontaminated by
the bourgeois shams of guilt, family and home;
but also a religious and political commitment –
each one-night stand a separate responsibility for life,
   and man.

I know too well the station where you picked him up,
   (or he
picked you), that fascinating messenger from ancient
   furies.
The gay guides are filled with places just the same,
where lust and destiny, danger and boredom all
come together in a final massacre of loneliness.

Una vita violenta – your own title
for the sad brutality of fallen Rome
that is for ever ancient, ruined by the scandal of
   perverse
papal prohibitions, by the moon's castrating goddess
who allowed a first and final grope, then
   excommunicated you:

crushed you to death in the suburban cruelty and
 moonless dark
of Ostia, pathetic substitute and shabby back-
 projection for
what should have been mysterious and scented pagan
 groves,
with high priests chanting, dancing, performing a
 forgotten rite
on naked Adonises, chained and ravished on altars of
 marble flowers.

– Instead, courageous and confessed comrade of boys
 and men,
compassionate Marxist-Sodomist of all male Christian
 love,
you in a pious odour of sanctity were hypocritically
 laid to rest
in Rome, according to the last rites of a church that
 you so often
both loved and lashed, celebrated and despised.

– Yes, they fucked up the final cut, and the unkindest.
But in the memories of men, you, Pier Paolo,
the close-up victim of your own compulsions, hero and
 villain
of your own divine poetic fantasies, forever cruise
infatuation's crowded boulevard of shadows

in your excessive chariot of love and death,
the moon-silvery Alfa Romeo, vehicle and property
of which your lonely genius and vision were the only
 stars,
and that you slowly faded out, in Ostia,
one Sunday night, in Scorpio, in winter, when the
 moon was dark.

Ecce Homo

Pier Paolo Pasolini: Report on an Inquest

When the body was found,
Pasolini was lying full-length,
face-down, one bleeding arm stretched out,
the other twisted underneath him.
His cheeks, so hollow in life,
puffed out by grotesque swellings.
His hair, sticky with blood, hung over
his scratched and torn forehead.
His face, punched out of shape,
was black with bruises, scored by knife wounds.
The hands, too, were pierced, with splintered palms,
and, like the racked arms, red with blood.
The fingers of his left hand
had been smashed, slashed.
The left jaw was fractured.
The nose flattened
and wrenched to the right.
The right ear half cut off,
the one on the left
hanging loosely, torn away.
There were stab wounds on the shoulders,
the thorax, the loins, with marks
made by the tyre treads of his car wheels
under which he had been crushed to death.
A horrible laceration
between the throat and the nape.
On the testicles,
extensive, deep bruising.
Ten fractured ribs, fractured sternum.
The liver ruptured in two places.
The heart burst.

(from *Corriere della Sera*, November 2nd, 1977)

Divina Commedia

The other day, Pier Paolo Pasolini,
one rainy February evening in Rome,
I retraced your final steps, your fall,
trying to make your martyrdom forever mine
upon the sad back roads of Ostia
whose grubby wilderness,
the streets and sands of Teorema,
the rocks and ashes of your perfect Passion,
drag on southwards into dusty dunes,
the railway tracks, the runways of Fiumicino –
aeroporto landscape of Fellini, Antonioni and Godard:
but above all, my Virgil, my deliverer, the common ground
of terrorism, torture, treachery,
of idle crucifixion, and lust in action.

Barbed-wire limbo of the destitute, the houseless,
a Caravaggio country of desire's final anarchy.
– Alone I roamed from one grimy station to the next
of our long Via Dolorosa, scarred and scattered
with scumbags, broken bottles, bones and dogshit.
There on my knees I prayed for some salvation,
wishing in that Gethsemane it had been only me
   you met that fatal evening in November –
not your Judas, but just your James, albeit James
the Lesser you picked up so casually about eight p.m.
where, so casually, about eight p.m., you picked up
me, some twenty years before, my comrade, at our common
rendezvous with fate – our last, pathetic calvary
of fools, piss-awful, the shitehouse at Roma Termini.

March, 1979

Pasolini Agonistes

He makes himself an easy target
for all those who gladly attack the weak
and so doing demonstrate
only their own puerility.

His transgressions many and varied.
The police have their dossiers on
every aspect of his personal life –
even his passion for playing football.

There are denunciations, not just
by the expected establishment authorities,
but also by friends and fellows –
poets, artists, actors, directors.

The ultimate judgment
is not the final or the only one,
but merely part of a trial subjected to
all his life, since a Friulian childhood.

Pasolini was always an easy prey, but
never a passive one. He offered himself unarmoured,
with total openness to guarded life, that meanly
took full advantage of such saintly innocence.

On Pasolini's 'Teorema'

Glimpsed in a courtyard, a gallery, a cloister, a
    garden –
yes, we know him all too well,
that plausible young male demon,
unscrupulous messenger of hell, fair angel of our fate,
handsome, mysterious, understanding,
and inexplicably loving,
who comes one day from nowhere
and takes our hearts, our minds, our souls,
our very names, in exchange for – what?

For loneliness and desolation worse than anything we
    knew
before his coming; for a persistent sense of loss,
an ache of separation, a bitter, loveless isolation
in a world to which he brought
a temporary joy, a passing sweetness.
– But was it worth it? A brief time
of unforgettable pleasure in a life of pain?

For now the pain grows worse,
the isolation more intense,
and he who came and took our souls
when we least needed him
does not come now, now that we need him most.

Instead, a hollow shadow walks beside us
and haunts us day and night
with visions, madness, dreams
of impossible and unimaginable love
that, even if we knew it once again,
we should reject, knowing it untrue
and foul; and unavailing, hollow
as the words and smiles with which
he first approached us, come from nowhere,
to take us back there with him, and leave us there
    alone.

City of AIDS

Under the earth, beyond the changing light
of normal day, the city never sleeps –
a city of dead gardens, plastic domes,
and streets converging only
on dank walls of dark.

In the sad illuminations of
unnatural day, the fevered lanterns
drain all colour from the pastel walls
of tenements and bars and small cafés,
and from the sick and painted faces
of the wandering inhabitants, all prisoners
wandering from room to room, from bed to bed
with restless eyes, like dreamers without sleep.

This is their ghetto, where they live
in idleness and grief, their sickness
sapping every energy but that of sex –
the clinics, hospitals, morgues, incinerators
are also the resorts of a despairing lust –
in sweating backrooms, dark as pitch,
in whistling toilets clammy as the grave
the lonely bodies cling, or grope their way
from hand to hand, from mouth to mouth.

All stricken with the same disease, acquired
in saunas, cellar bars, gay discos, furtive
movie houses or the porno peep-show, these
are the damned who copulate with death, their own,
knowing it does not matter whom they choose,
for every man becomes his own inverted messenger,
and also the receiver, of its phantom love.

A ceaseless throbbing music dulls the mind
with senseless repetitions, as they dance
to its reductive beat. Some kiss and coil,
some hold each other close, and some
dance lonely and apart, while others
shuffle in the dusty circles of tribal rites.

You who all your life had sought
that one pure love, that friendship of the soul,
can never find it here, where all are lost,
willing victims of impossible desires,
drugged invalids whose ineradicable sickness
can be traced to early youth, or passionate
childhood – the first, innocent embrace
of boy and boy, in the exciting darkness of the lane,
or far from the eyes of adults in the camp's deep
   woods,
the touch that seemed to spell the end of loneliness.
– Then shades of the prison house began to darken
that instinctive ecstasy with terror, guilt, betrayal,
loss of trust, of loyalty and tenderness and honour . . .

And now the only true release is death – release
from mockeries of life, and from the daily rumours,
seeping from above, of cures that never come,
or come too late. – O, careless love, what have you
   done?
Is this the final answer of the human heart?

Homo in Omnibus

(in memory of Sandro Penna)

The rush hour in Naples
lasts all day long, and
most of the night.

In the crowded bus,
the summer suffocated.
I tried to sublimate my agony

by gazing on a boy's delightful face
just out of reach, not out of mind –
that pure smile, those furry eyelashes!

While contemplating that *amour de tête*,
I gradually became aware
of a concern more close –

indeed, right behind me
an urgent male body pressing
with a policeman's truncheon.

I dared not look behind –
indeed I could not, my shoulders pinned –
but I could just insinuate my hand around

against the rough, worn cloth of someone's
cheap cotton working trousers
with its pocketful of change.

Not small change, either,
but something beyond price. I, too,
found myself in a manly condition

(as Nabokov puts it somewhere).
To be the possessor of such riches
in such a humble purse!

At Mergellina, I had to push my way
off the bus – and I was glad to find
he still was pushing close behind me.

On the station escalators,
I finally dared look round – and you
were there. You might have been

anybody, so ordinary did you look.
But you were laughing as your hand outlined
what I was now quite familiar with.

A few words, a handclasp, an offered
cigarette (refused), an arm in mine –
so we prolonged that first encounter,

so dangerously public, in hallowed privacy,
all night together in the small hotel he knew
near Napoli Piazza Garibaldi Termini.

It was an eternal one-night-stand,
a passing need, and none the worse for that.
But I have not forgotten our delight.

– And to my surprise, the hotel's name
was 'Sayonara' – a fitting one for a brief
encounter started between two stops.

Come Together!

'For the seed in their loins were hostile . . .'
   (W. H. Auden: 'Prologue': *Look, Stranger*)

Tenth Avenue, New York, in the steaming crotch of
the Meatrack, the gay saunas and the leather clubs,
the fistfucking backrooms and the SM torture
   chambers,
a sexual, medical and social revolution, man-to-man
on Christopher Street, on Christopher Street –
the Jerk-Off Joints, J.O. for short.

Acquired Immune Deficiency Syndrome finally
convinced them of the joys of masturbation –
bisexual, homo, het – what Onan was condemned for
became no more a sin, but rather, thanks to AIDS,
a healthy prophylactic pleasure, older than the hills:
for randy Adam practised it before the curse of Eve.

The graffiti-scarred phone booths of Washington
   Square
are full of fliers advertising private basement
   glory-holes,
where two or three, or more, are gathered, come
   together
in ritual self-abuse, all naked at the cellar bar, or
wearing only chest chains, a string, a jockstrap: in one
   hand
the member, in the other the 'Well-Come' drink – it's
   free.

'No Exchange of Body Fluids!' the tinsel notice says.
   'No
Suck, No Fuck!' and 'Only Cheek-Kissing Allowed!'
In a religious silence, only the concerted thumping
of a dozen engorged muscles on the job – this rhythm
a relief from the monotonous disco rock
and roll, the real headache of gaytrip nitelife.

Return to the tribal rites of troubled adolescence –
boys, pants down in a wanking circle, flogging it to prove
who had the biggest and the hottest head of steam, and who
could shoot it first and farthest in the musky, dusky barn,
the happy hayloft, the shower-room, the island sea-cave,
the timber-merchant's aromatic shed of shavings.

'Sex Without Danger!' Poppers and pills are out, but
pots of lubricating cream are sold across the counter
where the SM accessories and playthings gather dust – the slings,
whips, ropes, straps, gags, chains, leather gear.
At San Francisco, Fire Island, even in the Jones Beach dunes
the trend is 'Lend A Hand' in jerk-off joys of mutual masturbation.

So the high priests of once unspeakable practices, ardent devotees
of autoeroticism, self-pollination, formerly denounced and mocked
as infantile, or immature, or at the best unsatisfactory,
come now into their own, are seen now as the avant-garde
of feelgood grope, prophets, gurus of carnal knowledge, professors of
impassioned play, on Christopher Street, on Christopher Street.

Ode to Male Masturbation

Fantasia for the Right Hand
    'Atum the Egyptian sun-god rose from the
    primeval waters of the Nile, and, sitting upon
    a hillock of silt, abused himself, and out of
    his semen fashioned the other gods . . .'

What's this?
Down from a sky of pearly water
through a bathroom ceiling of broken
cloud and wind
descends
this enormous hand, cuffed in cumulus –
a hand – warm, strong but tender,
capable, comforting, concerned,
intelligent, and
with a mind of its own.

What horny-handed son of toil
now takes me in hand?
Slowly it begins to fumble with my flies
as if weighing up
the growing heaviness,
testing, divining the shape
of things to come,
the big boy's outline of history's
enormous gathering prick
that gradually stirs and rises
like the blunt nose of a jet taking off
lifting itself out of itself
out of a mist of hair
on two wheels
the jumbo tyres of my balls.

How heart-easing that first caress
of a strange hand
through the worn material
of corduroy, denim, leather!
I let him have his way.

He means to win the toss, it seems.
How masterful
this first light stroke,
then the insistent
pressure, as of a giant brush
loaded with hot oil
butting a throbbing canvas
with lashings of pure paint!

Then the great hand, disembodied
in its cuff of cloud,
tugs impatiently at the zipper's tag –
coyly reluctant, a little stiff –
that it hauls down like a flag
of utter surrender, a serpent hiss
that changes to a roar
of lightning and a flash of thunder!

Like a split pomegranate
my bulging codpiece
opens on a white gash
of crisp cotton underpants,
which the mighty hand at first
cautiously, gently explores
with two testing fingers only,
then suddenly plunders with eager fist
seizing and strangling my pulsing rod
whoops – have a care – right out in the open now –
cradling and dandling
the asymmetric balance of my balls
as pants fall helpless round my feet.

O, then
the whole hand
in all its vigour, heat and will
begins to coax
my cocked pistol, weapon
thrillingly dangerous,
and brought again and again
with spasm after choked spasm
to the verge of explosion –

But still the safety-catch is on.
O Jerusalem, let not my right hand
forget its cunning!
At any moment, if I wish,
I can release it, and let the godlike hand
race me and run me into rapture
to the music of despairing and exultant moans . . .

O great engine, now
I want to come, to come
all over queer, to come up and
free me some time . . . I've got to come
at last – my will
slips the safety-catch, the trigger
trembles on a hair-spring caress under the hand's
wise forefinger, while the thumb
grips the oozing barrel smoky with grease.

Shoot from the hip! Fire! Bang-bang!
A machine-gun hail of soft white bullets of blood
pulses down the undershaft – bang-bang
again, again, again, again, again –
the great fingers squeeze, tighten, arrest
the flow – then bang! – again – the final shot –
no – pausing only to reload the barrel
with another burst – again, again –
a softer bang, a last tremulous wang-wang
and at the end of the life to come
wanks off one final pearl of shot
which the blessed hand concernedly,
tenderly, passionately, slowly – ooh! –
wipes dry with a nice clean mansize handkerchief
of fresh Irish linen embroidered with green shamrocks.

Then, waving in a friendly manner
('Not goodbye, just *au revoir!*')
withdraws behind its heavenly cloud.

That was the Sun!
It'll soon be coming out again.

Hymn to the Foreskin

De causis fecunditatis gentis circumcisae.
Praeputium voluptatem in coitu auget, unde
faeinae praepuciatis concubitum malunt agere
quam cum Turcis et Judaeis.

True badge of all
workingclass lads
and out-of-work fathers –

costs too much to have it cut
when there's no money coming in.

Like father, like son –
he, too, was uncut, judging by
the glimpse I caught of his massive tool:
so he had me like himself.

And what richness I was left with!
I bless the hard times
that were against my circumcision,
and I bless my father's generosity.

*

Foreskin, praeputium,
forcemeat, pre-nuptial mass
of mothering fatherforthing –

fond hood, snug cowl,
big red riding blood,
cloak, scowl, lifted snout –

lips rosebud, pouted
in pleasure, stretched in
ecstasy, can be made
at any time
to widen in a pure
rounded smile

of wonder on
the heart-shaped ruby
of the seamless glans
revealing

not teeth, but
one winking eye
vertical

a joke
shared among the happy
few thus undoctored, un-
mutilated –
the original Adam
proud and clean, fresh
and hot as
new-baked bread,
far from the barbaric
bloody vision of
the tribal test,
the unrighteous rites
of circumcision.

The cruel tyrants
un-father figures
in the grove
the priests with knives
the stone block
stinks with gore –

mistletoe's milky beads
strung on the quick of
a bloody ejaculation
premature castration.

*

Manhood?
Mine is perfect
and intact –

(unlike Abraham's, who
had to perform the operation on himself
at the age of ninety and nine
Gen. XXIV, v).

Vir intactus –
One with the holy Hindu
whose sacred prototype
the lingam
can never be defiled by mutilation –
'an act of the greatest
and most unpardonable impiety'.†

*

Any loving hand
whether male or female
may retract
the thrilling veil, and view
the dewy rose,
glistening berry
on beds of straw.

How it glows
with banked and brimming
cusps of heat!
Empurpled, the horizon's zone!
It firmly lassoes
like a buttonhole
the gland's
engorged rim
is slung aslant
on stretched fretilla
like the rings of Saturn
or a funfair fishingrod's
luckydip loop
boop-boop bi doop
latching on to
pocket lamp or
bottle of pop –

Upon the verge of alabaster
a pillar's pediment
of crimson fruit,
deep as a root.
(No transplant or
unnatural graft
burdens this basket –
and the erect shaft
is a beaut.)

At its brimming base
this useless-useful
linking-loose
membership badge
and bandage
of bonding, of
fellow feelings.

*

O wild skin,
tender graft, so
easily ungrafted
without loss
of blood or sap, or
only a pearly driblet
of fore-cum –
dropped like a
hat or a shift or
a shawl
on the scrotum's
peachy flews,
or raised reverently
like pixie-hood or
mysteries of the caul.

Character-maker
and shaker:
emblem of the hypersensitive,
the gentle erotomaniac,

pulsing, passionate,
inexhaustibly driven
by motors of manhood –
blest battering-ram
of tenderness, truth,
compassion and concern.
Your owners are all
unmistakable – they are
the angels of lust and love
forever walking in our midst,
alone, unrecognized, except
by those who know.

*

As I still have my tonsils,
my adenoids, my appendix,
and all my teeth
(and hair)
I feel I am that rarity –
the whole man,
ideal of the Renaissance,
a Leonardo lad,
a Michaelangelo man.

No bloody execution
shall deprive me
of my kingly crown.

This is the only emblem
of brotherhood.
We who are thus
can recognize each other in the street
and greet each other
with a passing look,
like visitors from outer space.

†*Curiositates Eroticae Physiologiae; or, Tabooed Subjects Freely Treated* by John Davenport. London. Privately Printed, 1870.

Camping Out

Never having had anything in common with
life here below, I used to wear
stiletto heels with my Mackintosh tartan kilt,
black lipstick on my upper lip,
white on the bottom
(lip, I mean) –
violet fishnet elbow-length evening gloves
with colossal junk jewellery rings
worn conveniently on the outside.

Shaved my lissom legs right up to the navel
rimmed with opalescent rainbow paillettes
then painted a straight black seam
all down their slinky length.
My demure *poitrine*, my seductive *derrière*
powdered with minusculest sequins,
the three nipples rouged in contrasting tones
of stop – caution – go.

On my proud head with its flawless face
made up like a Picasso lady's
(when I don't have blue I use green)
what is both wig and picture hat, perfumed and
thermostatically controlled to suit the seasons.
And over all, flung with a gay abandon,
my mile-long scintillating feathered boa
imitating – nay, rivalling – the entire
sky at night, with numerous Milky Ways.

Thus clothed and almost in my right mind,
each inch-long fingernail a different hue,
I used to prepare each day to face
this ball-breaking existence some called life
mistakenly foisted upon us by some Almighty sod
in which – a virgin orphaned at the age of fifty –

with no fixed abode, no regular employment
and no apparent means of subsistence
I have always considered myself
to be nothing more than
patiently, elegantly, contemptuously
camping out.

Japanese Homomovies

In the dark basement cavern
few of the seats are occupied.
Most of the men and boys
seem to prefer to stand at the back,
out of the diffused glare of the projector's
ghost-ridden searchlight playing
on the intimate screen.

There, in radiant supernatural colour,
the crop-headed youths in jock-strap,
kimono, jeans or rustic breech-clout
parade their seductive bumps and bulges
in sauna, record shop, gay bar, gymnasium.
Together, drinking in the shower's bliss,
their open mouths, with puffy lips and
perfect teeth, crush in long-tongued kisses.

Or upon the judo hall's tatami floor,
in the love hotel's spotless toilet,
at strip shows or the live-act stage
they fall into each other's arms,
perform tender orgies in
the lush apartment of an older man,
who films them in close-ups
of every pant and penetration.

The dewy student is initiated by
a strict team captain, the maths teacher.
Or the tense, sex-haunted salaryman
sweating in a jam-packed suburban train
gropes for the first and only time
the helpless foreign visitor's swelling crotch,
while the American missionary just behind him
strokes the Fulbright scholar's boyish buttocks.

These all play out the imprinted fantasies
of those who, standing at the back,
have to make do with so much less –
the feather-light approach of fingers, then
the squeezed hands, interwoven knuckles,
palm massage, first gentle touch on thighs,
symmetrical explorations of erect anatomies –
the long, slow hiss of zippers and
the final battle throes with alien underwear
before the lights go up between the movies.
– And reality once more presents its ugly face
where unseen sex once reared its lovely head.

Narkissos

I am a dubious bisexual, in love
only with my own dear self. To me,
I am both boy and girl, both man
and woman, both eros and agape.

My mauve-tinted mirror
is my lake, unrippled by
any foreign hand or alien breath.
Perfection – an absence of others.

Unlike my classic brother,
I am no myth. That face –
this face – is mine: that body –
this body no one's but my own.

The full-length cheval glass
is my crystal coffin, that contains
my living self, completely,
my entire naked miracle of sex.

My dear Greek brother, you
tried to kiss your own reflection,
but found that your expectant smile
was borne away on mocking ripples

dissolving your ambiguous beauty
into an ungraspable enigma.
Your own gentle hands destroyed
what they loved best. You wept.

But I can press my lips upon
the dusty glass, and meet my own;
the kiss within this cup
at first is cold, but quickly warms –

the ideal slight reluctance
of the moody, half-willing lover
won passionately over to my will,
my fire – to become utterly mine.

I fold my arms around the tilting psyche,
thrusting rosetted chest, belly, loins,
my bevelled thighs, my heart-shaped knees
against that responsive figure in the room

beyond, through that transparent wall
that both divides and joins us.
We enter it, and leave it
as through a curtain of rainbow beads.

*

I draw back, in order to behold another
me – the warm outline of my body
breathed upon the crystal frame
that haunts me like a living ghost

or the impression on a shroud
in gay Torino – but my Veronica
is you, my lingering leprechaun,
who keep the admiration I admire

upon this mystic cloth of vision
that is indeed our looking-glass –
for you look out at me, and I
look in at you, look in at you,

trying to catch your eye, that somehow,
however close we come, evades me,
escapes you, and brings us to despair
without the shadow of a breath, a ripple.

All I Know Is

it's getaway day
but I have nowhere
nowhere to get away to

the only thing I know is I'm
packing an ancient suitcase
as if I were laying out a corpse

and the only thing I
know as I partake of
my poet's last supper –

bread, wine, after-dinner mints –
the only thing I know is
beyond the pale is where it's at

John McRae

As It Happened

•

Not I, But . . .
But, Of Course, He Said in Answer
12.30 a.m./5.30 a.m.
Looks
Lines
Gang Funeral
Earthquake
Opening
Motes Dancing
Bed Time: Story
For All My Lovers
Unsaid
Until Then Love
The Dear Love of Comrades
The Great Wank Poem
Unlove Poem
Celtic Song
The Tunkhannock Murders
The Cost of Living Like This
. . . not dead yet, yes, dead, good . . .
True Unreal
Seconds
Part
Against Dryness
Cats Smile

Introduction

'As It Happened' is also the work of an exile. These 25 poems tell it as it happened and evidence a love of language and literature. First collections often contain work which clearly shows the literary influences upon the author. The difference here is that such influences are wittily woven into the form and style of the poems, and the pleasure to be derived from reading them is not dependent upon knowing who or what the influence is. They stand on their own whilst acknowledging their past.

A sardonic humour, as in 'But, of course, he said in answer', runs through many of the poems. It is this humour combined with an intensity of mood and an immediacy, by which i mean the sense that the poem is happening now as you read it, that i identify as John McRae's particular voice.

In his best poems he makes the art of writing poetry appear to be very simple.

Martin Humphries
1986

Not I, But . . .

Ah, but please do not mistake that voice –
The fiction fictions speakers too.
Reader, not author, should make the choice,
So I am not me, he is not you.

Yet every story I tell is true.

> All writing is fiction
> Or becomes so with time.
> The facts become clouded,
> The details a sign
>
> That someone was writing
> For someone to read,
> That someone was speaking
>   not just to himself,
> Caring, not caring, were others to heed.

Let us go then, he and I,
And move among the voices false and true
– *My good friend, quoth I –*
as sure as I am I – and you are you –
– And who are you? said he.
– Don't puzzle me; said I.

But, Of Course, He Said in Answer

But, of course, he said in answer,
Images
Make poems.

Like yeast makes bread.

And, of course, he continued,
Autobiog-
raphical snatches

Are the hide and show of art.

Confession, of course, is
Self-indulgent –
All show, no hide.

The hide of the poet, tough, eh?

But, of course, he said in answer,
Sensitivity
Is all.

12.30 a.m./5.30 a.m.

12.30 a.m.	5.30 a.m.
Lights across the bay	Pink dawn behind Vesuvius,
Little left to say	That chill of held-in breath
A cracked voice, an old guitar	Which presages the beginning
An empty end to another day.	Of new brightness, beyond death.

These are the hours when the magic still lives.

Looks

Never write poetry.
Advice to a young poet.

I remember a night in Beaver, Utah.
Greyhound bus stop not even a station,

>three people two suitcases 8.40 p.m.
>*looking* straight at me

Describe it impossible, Jackson Mississippi easier,
>an empty station at least,
>a sleeping black being wakened by a junkie
>*looking* straight at me empty

Photograph of the Loire near Montlouis
Put it into words. Or Monet and his water lilies.
A Raffaello in the Pinacoteca in Bologna –
>one of the women, not a Madonna
>*looks* straight out at you. Look at *me*.

Write poems about the impossibility of writing poems.
Push images together and they might resound.
>>But nothing by chance, mind.

Or follow your own advice
Never travel by Greyhound.
Never did.

Lines

Every poet plagiarises.
If I say a cupful of incredibly warm sunshine
They'll know I stole it.

Yet here on the balcony,
Capri to the left of me, Ischia to the right,
Oranges growing below,

That's what I'm sitting in.
Who can be in dejection near Naples
And not plagiarise?

Gang Funeral

People ask about the Camorra.
It's not new.
It's mentioned in a Raffles story,
1899.

And it's not only here it happens.
It's anywhere
Personalities and power and cash
Combine.

It's that here the truth is nearer
The surface.
Religion and reality get along just
Fine.

Earthquake

So the earth moved.
It was always a joke till Sunday.

Sometimes, in indulgent moods,
I feel very close to death.
But never in moments of danger.

And now the earth moves again.
Another kind of danger
Another death
Passes into our ken
              And goes again.

Opening

'Weren't you on this train yesterday?'
Failed as an opening gambit
              because, as it happened,
I hadn't been on a train from Oxford to London
For something over two years.

But it wasn't intended literally, so I
              replied (truthfully)
'I didn't see you yesterday'

And things got under way.

It was only the following day, piecing
              together the love-chat
I realized, of course, that neither had he
Been on that train before.

              As it happened.

Motes Dancing

We only danced together once,
Close and touching
But moving not together

In light like a shaft of sunlight
That showed us who we were,
United momentarily
By the light, the place, the time.

The music gave us power,
Attraction grew to lust,
Erections in our pockets –
And the motes return to dust.

Bed Time: Story

'Andy would like to go to bed with you.'

When his lover tells you that,
Because the man's too shy to ask or try,
The reaction in you's mixed:

Has there been collusion? Is this one a voyeur?
Do they really want all three? And you?
Too flattered to say no, too embarrassed just to leap?

'To go to bed with you,' not, you note,
'You to go to bed with him.' Does this presume
A point of view, or, worse, a summing-up of you?

And if it never crossed your mind
Even to fancy him, does this new accessibility
Lend him qualities to desire?

Poor pander, to be distrusted so;
Poor Andy, where did your courage go?
Poor lovers, what is there left to know?
Do I, or do I not?   Don't know.

For All My Lovers

For all my lovers, for all my lovers,
I've never loved, for all my lovers.

I've met and wooed and won a few,
Who've now got lost between him and you,

And I've been taken, loved, and had;
Good times they seem now, more than bad.

But for all my love and for all my lovers,
I've never loved, for all my lovers.

It's physical and it passes time,
Makes some moments his and mine.
But I to him and he to me
Are never more than what we see,
Touch and go – and never more:
The search goes back to as before.

For all my lovers, for all my lovers,
I thank the Lord for all my lovers;
Gave away my heart and sold my soul –
But I pray the Lord, bring along some others.

Unsaid

'Would you tell David please
I'd like to suck his cock.'
It's the sort of thing that's at the top of your mind
And a moment behind your eyes wants to say it just to shock.

But in the company you'd want to say it in
You know you wouldn't dare,
And with the people who'd just laugh and chatter on
It's the kind of come-on that wouldn't get you anywhere.

Of course it might just be taken literally
If you had a little luck.
And all the thrill of conquest would be over in a flash:
You'd be left with a limp embarrassed version of something you didn't really even want.

Until Then Love

We always mean it – until we come.
It's only later that we notice how:
Where are those glorious moments now
The lying lips had sworn would last?
(Mozart knew it – he had a past.)

The pretending true is understood:
It is not, nor it can not come to good;
Creates a circumstance and dies,
Who could ever call it lies?

We always mean it, until we come –
Coming and going the familiar way,
Discarding the hoped-for lasting truth
That lies behind the things we say.

The Dear Love of Comrades

'Well, the least you can do is suck the boy's cock for him.'
    There's a kind of queenliness,
        you see,
    That puts itself above sex
        with equals.

'But I'm not gonna go to bed with a stupid queen like her' –
    Mentality that sets itself above
        the love
    And lovingness that there might be
        with equals.

'Just a piece of meat, not a thought in his head.'
        When
    'I would love just to see you naked'
        with equals
Should be the easiest, but is such a difficult thing to say.

The Great Wank Poem

You're not supposed
    to write
        (or read)
Poems about wanking.

But who would deny
    a good wank
        is better
Than a bad fuck any day?

Do you do it
    on your back
        or face down,
On yourself, or into something?

Have you tried it
    standing (on your feet!)
        in front of
Mirrors, or do you have some special fantasies?

Would you like to
    recall all the lovers
        you nearly had,
By name, and touch, and come with them?

Are they all imaginary
    or pictures from porn?
        Or do you see
No one – the grand abstract come?

How often do you wank?
    Or do you dislike
        that word, prefer
Masturbate, jack off, hand-job,

Do-it-yourself? Or pretend
    you just don't do it?
        I WANK
And love it. Move from questions now to answers.

I love it alone, or even watched,
    face down, into a towel –
        Kleenex falls apart,
The centre cannot hold a three-days' come;

And three is maximum: most straights
    and gays know that
        but don't admit it.
I come more often when I wank. Do you?

No need to worry about coming too soon,
    or even at all.
        Please only yourself,
No holding back, no 'was it all right?'

No talk or embarrassment
    get in the way –
        but that's just exactly
What you can't really say.

It would be nice if we could get
    through this taboo,
        and talk about
Wanking unselfconsciously,

Make it not an unsocial
    topic – not coarse;
        but loving ourselves
As our own intercourse.

Unlove Poem

But when you start a poem do you know
What it's going to say all the way through to the end?
And that's by no means the stupidest question I've heard.
My dear, sweet, ignorant child, just turn over and let
  me fuck you.
There'll be no love poems written for you.
                              But, then again,
I hardly imagine you reading any either. Have you ever
  read a poem,
Actually read one, properly?
                You make me catch a sudden glimpse
Of gaps and chasms.
                No, no, no, nothing's wrong. But
Who would ever have thought you'd make a poem come?

Celtic Song

I shall not betray my darling's name –
      Though Irish blood runs through his veins,
  Though English blood was shed in vain,
For no, he'll no come back again.

I shall not betray my darling's name,
      For woe to him who women defames;
  A woman or a man to him is the same,
And no, he'll no come back again.

I shall not betray my darling's name:
      The Tuatha De Danann are underground
  For there they stay forever young,
Emerge and touch, and back again.

I shall not betray my darling's name,
      King of my heart across the sea.
  A bonnie prince, his heart is free,
And no, he'll no come back to me.

The Tunkhannock Murders

I took this boy,
Peeled the skin from the back of his legs
Impaled him on a fence post,
Left him to die.

Another I just knifed
There and then.
The numbers grew quite quickly.
I wanted to frighten the town,
Wake it.
Make it different next year.

On the way from Buffalo to Scranton
It was fete day in Tunkhannock,
Fireman's ball, brass bands, parades
Blocked the road for an
                            hour
And
    twenty minutes.
What if there had been a fire?
Mindless village stops the world
To have its local party.

I had time to react, and raged.
People watched the parades. Some got in my way.
Tunkhannock returns to me
Every time I see such imposition
And am enraged.

I wonder would the funerals have
Blocked the traffic too?

The Cost of Living Like This

(to the memory of James Kennaway)

Well . . .
Yes . . . all right

I suppose I do regret –
But don't we all?
Not the things I've done, though,
No. More the things I wish I'd done

Could have been,
Chances I didn't take
Risks and follies, mistakes I didn't let myself make
And I won't get the chance to now.

Yes, all right, I suppose I do regret
– but don't we all?

Regrets, yes, I have regrets, dammit, but you don't let them get to you,
Do you? Everybody has regrets, don't go on about them. You can usually
Just ignore them. Dozen tiny failures
              Dozen unacknowledged disappointments
The usual barrage of not quite right
Every single day in life

If you hadn't asked
I wouldn't have bothered thinking about it . . .

No, that's not tears in my eyes,
Don't flatter yourself. Don't you realize
I'm driving against the sun,
My lenses have been giving me hell today.
You don't think you'd make me cry, do you? You?

It's the cost of living like this,
The price we have to pay for the life we choose to lead;
And it's never worth crying for the things you miss.
A strong indifference carries your hour of need.

Well . . .
Yes . . . all right

I suppose

. . . not dead yet, yes, dead, good . . .

Did he kill himself with work?
Did he kill himself with worry?
Would he cut his own hand off
And send it in a box
To his greatest enemy?

Are these the simple fantasies,
Are these the silly questions
That I ask, to come to terms
With a suicide that wasn't?

If we'd known we could have helped.
But we did and know we didn't.
Too difficult for us
As too difficult for him,
Myshkin sailing close to death,
Surviving to go deeper in.

Did we kill him with our ignorance?
Did we kill him with our love?
Would he give his heart
On a plate for us – and love
His only enemy?

True Unreal

The house I spent my early summers in
Took on, I don't know quite when,
But probably some three or four years
After my last summer there, something of

The Mill on the Floss. There is no monkey puzzle
Tree in the novel, that I can recall.
Bootscrapers outside the doors, maybe.
But a railway platform and booking-office
Instead of a river is the most surprising thing.

Still now if I lie in bed and hear trains even far off in
                                        the distance
It takes me back there – and back to the groves
And hunchback: certainly never there. Nor an orchard.
Big field, long grass, ladybirds, about which
I once wrote a story – all these, but no Tullivers.

Identification with a mood of years
Impresses real on true unreal.
It's all so intermingled clear
I never want to read the book again, for fear.

Seconds

'An interesting, odd, exciting volume.'
    Madge with a stone in her breast
Coming down the lane
    And a rather foul comment, out loud,
On the poet's incapacity and pain.

But the critical voice dispensing its sage
    Twists of disparagement
Shooting down in flames
    Takes little heed, nor should,
Of the difficulty of naming names.

Comings are seconds and thirds,
    Searchings to do it again,
Looking down the range
    Of ways and of wanderings of words,
And broken-voiced angels made strange.

So I forgive me for trying again,
    Old searchings, old shootings, old men;
Running down is fame
    In sniggers, in snatches, insane.
And that little Madge gives me, I claim.

Part

        Ah but we loved,
        There will always be that.

        Naked, almost embarrassed,
In an open green field
      A flitter of birdsong between
Our breath and our laugh.

        And late evening on Long Island.
The sand cold, the sea hushed –
        We were tiny and unique there:
The night sky is huger than the day.

      Yes, we loved, oh
Remember an open car in France
        And a kiss, a long kiss at speed
Through an endless road of poplars.

Some fumbles in the dark,
    To make secret love in others' houses,
To bare flesh quickly when someone might see
    Silent love and giggling love
    And open love
        and closing love

      But yes we loved
      and enjoyed our love.
      There's always that,

        And touching me
Unexpected like a splash
        Of crushing, gut-destroying,
Lusting love that quivers in your shoulder-blade

And loves.   That dies.

And loves.   Yes, that we had

Love   Yes, that.

Against Dryness

Do I, I ask myself frequently,
    do I have a Poetic Voice?

And I sometimes think, unsmiling, that I do.

Reading Cavafy, my lover elsewhere
    with his other lover, though,

I think jealousy and love have been done before

And if I take a little joy from a few
    brave poppies among the long grass down below

It can't match up with the hollow joy and dryness

That can only be expressed in the oldest words:
Unpoetically my love, my love, I miss you.

Cats Smile

Cats smile with their eyes.
    Not often, but sometimes yes,
Looking *to* you for a moment
    Instead of at you,
Meeting your eyes, holding the look
    An instant: a long blink
Is a smile.
        Followed quickly
    By disinterest, of course,
A yawn, a wash, a careless look around.
    But that was a smile.
And both of you know.

Gay Verse from GMP, the Gay Men's Press

DREAMS & SPECULATIONS
Poems by
Paul Binding & John Horder
ISBN 0–85449–039–6
64 pages   UK £2.95/US $5.95

THREE NEW YORK POETS
Poems by
Mark Ameen, Carl Morse &
Charles Ortleb
ISBN 0–85449–052–3
to be published in 1987

FIVE BLACK POETS
Poems by
Dirg Aaab-Richards, Craig G. Harris,
Essex Hemphill, Isaac Jackson &
Assotto Saint
ISBN 0–85449–053–1
to be published in 1987

NOT LOVE ALONE
Martin Humphries (ed)
Anthology of gay verse
by 30 modern gay poets
ISBN 0–85449–000–0
144 pages   UK £3.50/US $6.50